MEISTER ECKHART'S
Book *of* Secrets

MEISTER ECKHART'S
Book *of* Secrets

Meditations on Letting Go and
Finding True Freedom

MARK S. BURROWS AND JON M. SWEENEY

HAMPTON ROADS

Cover art: Brother Pedro Machado (d. 1604), by Francisco de Zurbaran,
(1598-1664) © Real Academia de Bellas Artes de San Fernando,
Madrid, Spain/Bridgeman Images
Typeset in Truesdell

Hampton Roads Publishing Company, Inc.
Charlottesville, VA 22906
Distributed by Red Wheel/Weiser, LLC
www.redwheelweiser.com

Sign up for our newsletter and special offers by going to
www.redwheelweiser.com/newsletter/.

ISBN: 978-1-57174-847-8

Library of Congress Cataloging-in-Publication Data
available upon request

Printed in the United States of America
IBI

CONTENTS

INTRODUCTION

There is a secret hidden within each one of us. Meister Eckhart knew this, and never tired of speaking about it—in sermons delivered before ordinary people, for special audiences of cloistered nuns, and in the intellectual halls of his day. What is this secret? It is many things, and it is nothing at all.

The secrets that Meister Eckhart speaks of are similar to ones that Jesus alluded to when he taught the parable of the hidden treasure and the parable of the pearl of great price. In the first tale, a pilgrim discovers treasure hidden in a field and immediately seeks to purchase that field. In the second, the pilgrim discovers a pearl of great price, "went and sold all that he had, and bought it." But, of course, these secrets aren't really for sale.

No one can buy what's spoken of here. On the contrary, to discover these secrets, one must be willing to give up a great deal. There's giving up, for instance, the effort we expend trying to build up a self-image. There's giving up the need to justify ourselves. There's letting go of everything we thought we had, in order to hold on to what actually gives our lives meaning. If this all sounds intangible, that's because it is. But it is no less real for that.

When it comes to the treasure upon which our worth depends, the "pearl" that finally matters, the work before us is not that of accumulating, which is so much part of our consumer culture, but rather that of letting go—of what we think we need to make sense of things. For much of this is finally little more than a barrier to the very thing we most desire: contentment, peace of mind, rest in our heart. The Meister knew about this, reminding us that the "secret" to such things is generally out of reach only because we have sold our soul to bidders who cannot deliver what they promise: true freedom. Or what we once spoke of as soul freedom.

What is this freedom? It is the open secret of our true nature, that within us is the treasure, the pearl of great price, buried in the field of our lives. And that *we* are the only ones in a position to let go of what we do not need to gain this treasure, opening ourselves to the true self that was within us from the beginning.

Eckhart knew much about this as a Dominican friar, often called upon to teach students in Paris and Cologne as well as preaching to congregations far and wide, including many in the convents of the province of Thuringia and later Saxony, which he served as provincial. He was tireless in speaking of our essential nobility at a time when much of the church's rhetoric gave little attention to this ancient wisdom. One of his favorite themes, which had become something of a secret in the hands of many theologians and preachers of the day, was that each of us has what he called a "noble soul." No, more than this: that each of us *is* such a noble soul, and that this is the pearl of great price that lies in our heart.

This inner self—or "ground," as Eckhart often called it— is the one treasure God desires us to find, a gift given at the beginning that abides within us all along this "pathless path," to recall his image. The journey of discovering this "way" happens when we open our hearts to embrace it as our true self. For this reason, freedom of the soul is not an ambition for something beyond us, but rather a gift we carry within ourselves. It is the treasure in our heart that lies in wait for us to find. When we do, we discover that we are nothing less than the very image of God, and that we and God are finally one.

This seems so simple. But it is not necessarily an easy path to follow, as those know who have lost themselves in the hurry and worry of their lives. Does this mean that we should resign ourselves to doing nothing, a resignation that in olden times was denounced as the heresy of quietism? By no means, according to Eckhart. But we must be careful to remember that the discovery of this treasure is not one more achievement we can manage. It is not something we do. It has more to do with undoing, letting go of our need to manage our lives, freeing ourselves to seek this treasure—and coming to see that it waits for us in every moment.

How do we find the courage to do this? That, too, is a kind of open secret, as the Meister knew: it requires relinquishing our desire to know about what we might gain. What it depends upon is our willingness to lose what we thought was necessary to give us worth in our lives. We must "die" to that self if we hope to discover our noble self, which is the "ground" of our lives. As he once put it with characteristically paradoxical language: "Now as the soul loses herself in all ways, she finds that she is herself that same thing which she has sought without success." In this experience, he goes on to say, "the soul knows her own beauty." Which is what we hope for, beneath the surface of all our restlessness, our insatiable hunger for things, our seemingly endless desire to find meaning, and the depletion that comes of all this.

All of this has developed a quite lucrative spiritual market in today's world—with a seemingly endless offering of self-help books and seminars, some to have on the cheap, others costing a pretty sum. But at the end of the day, the secret is this: to find yourself, you must lose yourself, letting go of what you thought you needed. This is the path that ultimately leads to true freedom. Jesus said it, again and again, and so did Meister Eckhart in his sermons and writings. Our renderings of his thought give voice to his wisdom in the poems that follow.

If this is what you yearn for, if this is the "pearl" you are willing to sell all you have to find, Eckhart's wisdom might be the royal road you are seeking. Even if it seems daunting, it will be a wager worth trying. For if Eckhart is right, these secrets are the treasure that promises nothing less than true freedom and fullness of life.

♦ ♦ ♦

Finally, then, a word about the form of the meditations gathered in this volume. Meister Eckhart wrote within the expected parameters of theological discourse in his day, at least in terms of their outward form: sermons, both in Latin and German, academic texts addressing disputed questions in the schools, and edifying treatises composed for his Dominican confreres.

But his thought was profoundly poetic, even if he did not venture into the formal domain of poetry. The poems found here, then, are not his, at least not strictly speaking. As with our earlier book, *Meister Eckhart's Book of the Heart*, these take the form of short meditations on the audacious and often paradoxical wisdom found in his writings. They are often quite close to the language and images found in his writings, but they "translate" his closely argued and often complex prose into more spacious poetic form. In some cases, phrases or whole lines are taken verbatim from his texts, though more often they carry the texture and momentum of his thought, borrowing the essential thought-pattern found in his texts but rendering them as meditative poems.

Our hope is that we have conveyed dimensions of his thought in a form accessible for modern readers. In this sense, one might understand this as a "carrying over" of his spiritual insights and intellectual musings into modern English, which after all is what translation, in its Latin root, suggests. We trust that they re-present his thought in ways that communicate his genius for readers for whom the style of his writings might not be easily accessible.

For those who wish to trace the arc of this "translation" process, we have included endnotes pointing to the texts that inspired these poems. Our hope is that those who wish to pursue Eckhart's thought might be able to turn back to these original sources, not simply to check on the poems' authenticity but to engage more deeply the inner texture of his mind—and ours.

....

It was no accident that his earliest admirers referred to him as the "Meister," a gesture of respect and even veneration by those who were astonished if also at times baffled by the startling audacity of his teachings. Our hope is that these poems might invite readers into the secrets of this wisdom, one which draws on perennial truths that point to what Eckhart called the "pathless path," which alone can lead us into true freedom.

Prologue: There Is a Secret Hidden in the Heart

There is a secret hidden in the heart,
a treasure as close to us as our breath,
a mystery living in the midst of our soul.

Finding it is simple, but may be hard,
since to do so we must abandon the self
we thought we were and seek the gift

that is always ours: this inner spark
that no darkness can finally extinguish,
though it keeps us from knowing it.

This gift is always present to us, if only
we have eyes to see. And when we do,
we will find its radiance in everything,

and at all times, this light that blazes
on in a darkness that cannot put it out,
this secret that finds us when we risk

abandoning ourselves to this presence.

Part One

SEEKING LIGHT

Even in the Shadows

Even in the shadows of my life
where I often tremble with shame,
You are present there as the light
that ever shines without ceasing,
and when I turn my heart to that
darkness I find that You were
there, shining, all along.

God Is Green

Your pure soul is
untouched by its flesh,
unbound by its time,
exclusively for God
who is green and flowering
with all joy and power.

If You Could See

If you could see
just for a moment,
a split-second in time,
the eternally green,
birthing power of God,
you would not be
able to recall your
past and present
suffering and pain.

God's Now

We cannot see everything.
Yet everything is there
in a single light.
Unchanging eternity is its name.
If you could see it,
or simply be in its glow,
nothing would ever pass away.

The Inner Eye

Are you looking for God
using the same eyes you employ
to perceive temporal things?
That won't work.
God is not like colors in the sky.
What you see with
those old eyes of yours
is something else.
It is not God.

Just for a Moment

> If you could see
> who you really are
> for only a moment—
> you would see your life,
> and all life, pure being,
> nobility and givenness,
>   perfection.
> You would never, then,
> turn away again.

God's Gaze

There are
of course
millions of
people and more
but know
that when
God looks
on one of
them, alone,
that one
receives
everything necessary
from that
singular gaze.

A Great Light

"There was a very great light,"
the scripture says, for when
Wisdom comes into the mind,
when a soul finally comes to rest
from its passions and concerns,
there also comes a quiet silence
as that soul rests from its spinning,
with new understanding.

Received

It is wicked
to expect
some specific
thing from God.

If you asked,
you received—
and received in full,
more than you
can imagine or
know.

Follow Me

People seem to respond
in three ways when Christ says,
"Follow me":
those who run ahead
are wicked;
those who remain close by
are missing an opportunity;
but those who truly follow,
they are perfect.

To Be Satisfied with Hell

If you are so present in God
that your will and God's are the same,
you wouldn't so much mind
sickness over health,
or pain over happiness.
You would even be satisfied with Hell,
if that was where you and God
were going together.

Did You Ever Wonder

Did you ever wonder
what the greatest gift is
that God has ever done?
It is this: mercy.
If you wonder
what this means,
practice mercy
and your questions
will fade. Live into mercy,
and you will become
what you love,
for love unites us
in our loving,
not in our being.
So give yourself
to love, and love
yourself in giving.
The rest will follow
of its own.

Rotten Eggs and Brown Apples

To love God is to consider
that what God wants as good
and godly is important in your life, too.
So, don't imagine yourself too clever,
so fresh and so original
that you end up throwing what
God wants out the back door like
rotten eggs and brown apples.

An Honest Prayer

I love you,
you see,
I do.
And I want
what you want,
but honestly,
more than that,
I wonder,
could I convince
you to change
your mind?

Intentions Matter

Don't be like the falcon
that hovers over
the woman with
a bundle of sausages
walking home
from the market.
That falcon follows,
but not as Christ
says to follow to
those who would
love him.
Intentions matter.

Yes, Darkness

I
Everything glorifies God
in its own way.
Yes, darkness, too,
the one out there
and the one that
hides within me
in my difficulties
and tribulations.

II
And what, after all,
would God be
without it—
for it is where
God wants to be,
so that light
can have its way
with me and
my darkness.

Ours Is the Darkness

I
Ours is the darkness
that seeks the light,
and God's is the light
that longs for the dark.
It's a simple equation,
even when it isn't so
simple.

II
So welcome what
comes of the dark.
Greet it as another
possibility where
the light might
shine again.

The Sheep's Eye and Mine

My eye has more in common
with a sheep grazing on the far side
of the sea, which I have never seen,
than it does with my own ears.

How can that be, you ask? Well,
the sheep's eye shares with mine
the capacity to see, which my
ear knows nothing about,

and hearing is unmoved by light.
But the uncreated light alone
is what wakes the soul from
the darkness of its slumber.

Seek God in Nothing

If someone tells you that God is here or there,
pay them no heed. And if they tell you that God is
this or that, ignore them. For you will only find
God when you remove every something and
seek him in nothing, and you will only see
him when you become blind and remove every
something from him. If you do this, you will
finally have only God, and God will have only you.
This is what matters; the rest will take care of itself.

Pay Attention to the Nothing

"Paul rose from the ground, and with eyes open saw nothing."

Acts 9:8

I
Pay attention to the nothing
the apostle saw with open eyes.
And consider what a wonderful
word this *nothing* is. What does
this mean? I say that it could
mean any of four things:
> first, he saw the nothing that was God;
> second, when he got up, he saw nothing but God;
> third, in all things he saw nothing but God;
> and fourth, when he saw God, he saw all things as
> nothing.

II
Which one of these is true for you
depends on how you look,
not what you see.
So pay attention to this nothing
in the way you look,
and in everything find God with
> open eyes!

....

Find the Inner Eye

We see in two ways, because the soul has two eyes.
One is an outer eye, beholding all that is creaturely
around us, all that we can see in the outer world,
all that we can imagine among things that change.

We need this eye to manage from day to day, and
moment to moment. But the eye that really matters
is the inner eye that beholds what is beyond change.
When you retreat from what is outside of you,

you'll taste what true freedom means; not that you
will have no more troubles, but all this will no longer
bother you. What to do? Find the inner eye and learn
to see your life entirely with it. The rest will follow.

If You Want to Reach the Highest Wisdom

If you want to reach the highest wisdom,
refuse everything you know, abandon all

you aspire to be, and seek the darkness of
the lowest place of all. Become nothing,

and there God will pour out the whole
of himself, who is All, with all his strength,

and you will see in the light you long for.

Becoming Peace

I
What is the heart of lasting peace in our lives
and for our world? Simply this: the realization
that what God accomplishes in the only-begotten
God does in each one of us as well, so that we
might become this beloved one.

II
To what end? So that we might learn to love
ourselves, and as we do this, as we learn to love
ourselves for who we truly are, we cannot
but love everyone else in the same manner.
This is the source of the wisdom whose end is
the peace we were meant to become, which
is beyond our understanding but not beyond
what we long to know in our experience.

Think Again

If you thought evil erases
the good, think again:
what prevents you
from seeing it there
might just have to do
with the way you
are looking.
Look again, for it
shines even there,
at least for those
with eyes to see.

A Wide Wilderness

You will not find me
in the usual places.
Come to the desert if you'd
like to see.
Look where you might
become lost for a while.
There is a wide wilderness
in me.

Enclosed

To find God
is to go nowhere.
Angels suddenly
appear in your path;
never mind them.
To find God
is to go where
we are alone
with the One,
enclosed.

Four Kinds of Ecstasy

A first ecstasy comes with intention,
when we reject the world's pleasures for God.
     This is love.
A second ecstasy comes with imaginative vision,
when we see, apart from our senses, God around us.
     This is spirit.
A third ecstasy happens beyond sense and imagination,
when we see God in the mind, by infused and holy grace.
     This is like the "deep sleep" of Adam in the Garden.
Then, there is a fourth ecstasy,
when the mind's eye can truly see God.
     Of this I will say no more.

What You Know with God

What you know with God
is what God is.
There is nothing better.

You will see infinity,
simplicity,
wholeness,
depths,
love,
purpose,
One.

There is, for you,
nothing else.

Part Two

FACING DARKNESS

To Someone with God

To someone with God,
there is happy discomfort,
there is glad darkness,
there is joyful grieving,
there is a lack of nothing;
and that lack, that nothing,
is otherwise hard to find.

Where We Are

When you are really free
you will no longer pine away
for freedom;
you will be present in
this moment;
you will be happy to follow
God alone in the light
that shows us
where we are.

Blessed Are the Martyrs

Blessed are the martyrs
who suffered for the name of God.
Some say,
    Life is short.
    Live it and don't be afraid.
Others,
    You should be dead already to
        what the world finds important.
Both are true.
Both life and death are your salvation.

Between Two Darknesses

If darkness is at the beginning, then it is
also at the last end. Don't be surprised by this,
for God rests there in the hidden darkness
of his eternal divinity, where he is unknown
and remains unknown as he is in himself.
Do you think it is any different than this
in your darkness, between these two?

No Matter How Deep the Darkness

No matter how deep the darkness
within you, there remains a spark
there, and this light wants only this:

the naked God as God truly is, and
not ideas about God, however true
this might be. This spark wants

the deep ground that is God—
the quiet desert, the simple silence.
And there, in this innermost place

beyond knowing and being, there
the spark desires what it needs,
and finds what it desires.

Picture the Knight

He leaves home,
risking everything he has,
traveling to faraway places,
danger on every side,
seeking a bit of passing glory.
We are not knights,
because the glory we seek
will never pass;
so why do we complain?
Why do we see this journey
and regard the risks
so dearly?
They are as nothing.

Whatever It Is

Whatever it is
that lives and breathes,
or loves and seeks
meaning or love
in return,
is loving after
God, without whom
there is no existence
at all.

Try Emptying Yourself

Empty a cup completely and keep
it empty so that not even air can
enter inside.
If you can, that cup may cease to
be a cup at all.
So, you might try emptying yourself
of cares and things, of all that
now fills you, and you, too,
might become something new.

If You Want to Find the Truth

If you want to find the truth that matters,
remember this: it's hidden and not what
you think. So stop thinking. And don't
imagine you can find it through what
you can put into words. It's like light
that bursts forth from the darkness,
like waters rising from unseen depths,
or the wind that blows where it will.

If We Could Ever See

If we could ever see, if only for a moment,
the delight and joy that are in God, we

would gladly embrace the darkness
that comes to us, considering it of little

worth, even as nothing, so great would
be the measure of our joy and pleasure.

Your Notebook Jottings

Imagine a soldier, with the finest arms available
hanging in a closet, never worn.

Just as useless as those weapons
are your notebook jottings about being virtuous.

You have to put virtue on
for it to come to mean anything at all.

A Mirror

Stay close now,
do not go far from here,
for God is only as close
as a mirror,
and if it falls, so
falls the image that
once appeared
there.

In Dark Times

In dark times, even
in death, we do well
to remember that

for God nothing
is ever lost or gone,
not even in death,

since God holds
everything that is,
even death itself,

in the eternal Now
of abundant love
and endless blessing.

We Cannot Know What God Is

We cannot know what God is,
but we can imagine it like this:

it is a greening and blooming,
a burning and glowing, a pouring

forth of love without measure,
a meeting of dark suffering with

the light of pleasure, a mingling
of earth with heaven, a delight

that exceeds what we can ever
know while remaining within

the bounds of what we can
imagine and surely hope for.

Some Imagine There Is No Light

Some imagine there is no light
in their life but only a long darkness.

I say that the light is never absent,
always seeking to flow forth within
the ground of the soul, but we block
it in our confusion and fail to see
how it ever shines and burns in us.

So if you want to know the light,
you must first face the darkness
that is in you. Only then will
this light overflow your soul and
dance with radiance in your life.

Anger or Peace?

> If you want to seek light,
> pay attention to the darkness
> within you, which is your anger.
> And when it rises up in you,
> let it go, for if you choose
> anger, you'll find that God
> stays far away from you,
> for as much as you lack
> peace, you will lack God.

Learn to Become God's Joy

Some truths are as remarkable as they are simple,
and this is one such truth: God's nature is to give

and give and give, without measure, and God does
this at all times—but especially when we are down

and out, lost and lonely; God asks only that we take
what comes in this gift, which is nothing less than

God's very self, and when we refuse to do this
we deny who we are and, finally, kill God.

So open yourself to this gift and ready yourself
for this truth and so learn to become God's joy.

This Truth Is All that Matters

This truth is all that matters, but it's hid
deep in darkness, a mystery so great
and sublime that no words can hold it.
So empty yourself of what you thought
you knew about it, and trust the silence
at the beginning and end of thinking.
This is where God waits to find you,
the pearl of such great price that you
must forget what you know and sell
all you have to acquire it. Once you do,
it is all you need. Nothing else matters.

One Love

If you seek God with prior expectations, you might get
what you expect, but you'll know nothing of God—

because God always hides in the dark of our knowing.
But if you seek God without any idea about who or what

God is, you'll find yourself one with the One, and in
this light find yourself joined to the One who

is always Love, without beginning or end.

Among the Miracles

I
Among the miracles ever happening among us,
the greatest is this: that God is ever glowing

and burning with all his riches, in all that is—
in every darkness we face and in all that we

must suffer and endure. And God does this
constantly and without ceasing, opening to us

in just this way a measure of his sweetness
and the abundance of his good pleasure.

II
This, too, is a miracle, for we can never exhaust
these riches or speak of them adequately,

and in this knowing we find the power
to face the burdens of each day and every

new hour, this gain more than we deserve
but not more than we need, and in this

knowing we embrace whatever is to come
in our lives of suffering and of pain.

If You Were So Holy

If you were so holy
you would not need God
at all and your work would
leave you calm and confident.
If you were so holy
you would be imperturbable
when others try turning you
away from God's presence.

Who Can Understand This

Who can understand this: that God
is creating the world not out there,
but in the innermost part of the soul,
where there is no time nor the light
of any image?
If you imagine this,
you will know—if only in a small way—
that even in the darkness you are no
more separate from the world than
God is.
And if you glimpse this,
even if for a moment, you will know
that God is becoming human again
and again, even now, even in you.

Some Say God Is Gentle

Some say God is gentle and kind,
but I say we only truly know this
in the abyss of the godhead where
we taste the abundance of God in
the darkness before the first day
and in the image of his whyless love.

So take leave of God for God's sake,
and dare to dwell in that single
oneness beyond every hope of gain,
where nothing separates you
from God.

If It Is True

If it is true, as the Scriptures say,
that God made the heavens and
the earth, then it is also true that
God is still making all that is—
the many from the one, light
out of the darkness, and order
from chaos. So take heart and
dare to break through, if only
for a moment in your thinking,
and set aside what troubles you.

Imagine this Amazing Truth

Imagine this amazing truth:
God is always creating within
you, in the heart's darkness,
amid the shards of your life
and even in the chaos. Even
there, God *is* and you *are*, in
the perpetual Now that is
Love in and through you.

You Ask, What Is Evil?

It is the good turned round,
deprived of what matters,
of all that really endures,
of all roots,
of what remains after a fire.
It stands outside,
pointing away, dividing,
fallen, falling, broken.
There is always evil lurking in
the good.

Removals

Look for it.
The Baptist cried
in that wilderness,
"Prepare the way!"
You must know
you must know that
the only sure way of
removing every obstacle
to God comes through poverty.
You have to be, have to be, naked.

Your pride, Eckhart

is the root of all your sin.
You leave undone what needs doing,
having better things to do.
And then there is what you do—
need I remind you?
But remember, man,
the *humus*, that ground
out of which you were formed.

Part Three

RISKING LOVE

May I Be Struck Dead

I have heard of people so frightened
by what they see is about to happen
to them that they fall dead on the spot,
and the attacker goes on by.
I believe joy can work that way too,
when one sees God who is coming
not as an attacker but as one who
is just as suddenly upon us.
The soul shrieks and dies
of that so-joyful fright.

Gather the Treasure

There are those who say
their meditation and prayer
are so good that nothing more
is necessary. Not so, Eckhart.
Saints only become saints
by practicing virtue. Your
eternal happiness may feel secure,
but what about others?
Even Christ spent a lifetime
about that work.

Sleep for a Century

Spiritual teachers say,
go to sleep now,
for a long time.
How about even one
hundred years?
Maybe then, you will
have forgotten the images
and the occupations that
seem to fill you. Maybe.
Maybe then you will be
able to sense what God is
doing inside you. Maybe.

We Are All Virginal

We are all virginal
when we receive God in us.
It is so sweet to have him,
but far sweeter it is to be
made fruitful by him.
And when that union becomes
a gift for others, it is clear—
this is not only for ourselves.

You Should Really Know

You should really know
that no one has given up
so much as to have
nothing left to give up.
And only insofar as you
let go of things and
abandon what you
think is yours
will God enter with
all that is God's.

May Your Will Be Done

We say these words all the time,
don't we, in the Our Father?
But we miss the meaning
of the familiar prayer
most every time we say it.
We imagine that the task
is to wish God's will be done,
when it really is to wish that
my will, all will, be God's,
but this only happens when
I get completely out of
the way.

This Is God's Prayer

That you have my grace,
that you desire my grace,
that you at least desire to desire my grace,
given freely and abundantly;
that this will be your desire,
so that I might be born in you,
amen.

Sweet Fruit

When you learn to love to practice the virtues
of love, hope, faith, courage, justice—then
you come closer and closer to God.

Your love for virtue is a love for God,
but it is even more than that.
Your love for the virtues is how you may,
one day, taste God's very sweetness, because
God is the sweet fruit of holy obedience.

An Angel's Joy

Some people wonder
whether the joy
is less for those
angels who live here,
among us on earth,
than it is for those
who dwell in heaven.
I say, their joy is the same
because joy comes
in doing the will of God
wherever you are.

Why Love Is Best

The God who is "I am who I am"
is also, so simply, just "love."
So, from the first,
everything has its
existence in this God,
who is better called love,
for that love spreads,
diffusing everywhere,
unifying us,
all in one.

The Best Thing about Love

I
What is the best thing about love?
That it compels me to love God. But detachment
is even better than this, because it
turns me from clinging
to the things of my
life until finally only
God is left.

II
So practice letting go, and then
let go even more, making room
for God to love you, not for your
love and not for your good works,
because your letting go frees
you to love God, and it is this
that compels God to love you.

Heavenly Now

We are all born at the right time.
We live, outward and earthly,
day by day in the sacraments,
until death, in the hope of heaven.
But all this is possible, and more, for
those who live a different kind of life,
in whom God shines, inward and
heavenly, now.

God Is Not to Be Found in Any Way

So you want to learn to love God?
Well, there is no particular way,

since God is not to be found in any
way. Try this: love God in a way

beyond every way, and, if you love
as nobly as you can, you'll find

that every way is the right way.
If this is enough for God, dare to

believe that it is enough for you!

Pray for Me

People often come to me
and ask me to pray for them.
When they do, I think to myself:
Why abandon who you are?
Why not remain in your self
and draw from the deep
well of your own good?
For each of us holds all
the truth in ourselves.

The soul that is yours

is yours only,
and precious,
unique,
of noble substance,
known by God,
loved unconditionally
by God the way
one loves one's
own self.

One in the One

One often hears it said
that love joins all that is
as one, but I disagree.

No, all that was and is
and will be, all this is
already one in the One

who is Love without
beginning or end, and
when we love, we

become one with One
who is the beginning
and the way forevermore.

Have You Tasted?

Have you tasted
the sweetness of God?
Have you tasted
the joy of heavenly things?
—the eternal pageant that
is available to you now?
This wilderness you now see
is nothing compared
to the Real Sweetness.

What We Love We Become in Love

A wise teacher once said that what we love
we become in love, so when we say that we
love God, do we mean that we *become* God?

At first blush, this sounds outrageous, and it is,
but it's no less true for all that, for in the love
we give—to God or to others—there are not

two but one, and in love you are more God
than you are yourself, for what you love you
become in love. So love—and let the rest be.

Why Would You?

Would you ever attempt
to carry a ton of iron
or lead, or even potatoes,
for that matter?
How impossible!
You would have to have
some help.
But the truth is this:
Your load is possible with help
from One for whom strength
is beyond measure.

The Value of Gold

How good is the one who donates
a thousand pieces of gold
to build churches and monasteries!
How wonderful the one
who is able to look upon
those gold pieces as having
no worth at all!

What Is Freedom?

What is freedom?
  To love God without asking why.
What is joy?
  To live in the freedom of God's unity.
What is life?
  To taste the love that lives in the heart.
What is hope?
  To know that God gives birth to me in the Spirit.
What is love?
  To realize that God is one and I am one in this One.
What is freedom?
  Not merely to know all this, but to live it out day by day.

God Is Not Far Away

God is not far away,
St. Augustine says.
So, if you desire
nothing to keep
you from God, then
submit yourself to what
God wants for you.
Simple.

Solomon Says

Solomon says
all streams run
to the sea
and return to
their source.
These waters are
like our souls
that run like streams
to the One
who is
drawing them
Home.

How Should We Seek God?

I
Some wonder if this is possible,
since God is incomprehensible, but
I say it can be done in three ways:

first, in all other creatures that exist;
second, in all the things we do;
and third, with flaming love.

Give yourself to these three
and you will find what you were
seeking on the wayless way.

II
When you seek God like this,
don't try to grasp it in words, since
love is beyond our grasping—

but not beyond our experience.
There, you will find the wayless way
that leads you into God's very self

where you are brought to wonder
in the unity of that blissful eternity
which rests in you and in all that is.

Forget about Being Spiritual

I

Forget about being spiritual if you want
to love God properly, and try loving
without regard for God's loveableness,
because God is above every notion of love—
and in this sense is not loveable.

II

How, then, should we love God?
Forget about being spiritual, and work
at becoming simple. Unite your life.
Only then will you know what it means
to love God unspiritually, because God
is not spiritual. God is One, and in
this oneness dare to sink down
out of every *something* into
the *nothing* that is God.

There Is a Comfort in Suffering?

There is a comfort in suffering?
This is true.
So it's said in the Gospels.
And we know it, too, in
the natural light of reason.
What is it but this:
When the uncreated God is
your father, nothing on earth
can really harm you.

This is difficult, Eckhart

but it is also true: Every
pain we feel
comes from our love
of things that loss
has robbed us of.
Pain happens when I give my love
and my heart to creatures and things
rather than to God alone.

Don't Be Like King David

Don't be like King David who,
knowing God was not
yet living fully in him,
complained in a Psalm:
"My tears have been
my food day and night,
while they say to me
all the day long,
'Where is your God?'"
Those healing but sad
tears.

Into the Fire

I
Watch a Spark as It Kindles

Watch a spark as
it kindles on dry wood,
receiving and
succumbing
with pleasure,
becoming fire,
forgetting what
it was,
engulfed.

II
You Will Be Empty and Bare

You will be empty
and bare
the closer you come
to God.
Don't be afraid.
As your soul looks,
and God looks back,
this is love like
a fire.

III
Those Other Things

Those other things
that keep you
from drawing toward
the Holy One,
what are they?
They are unlike
who you really are.
They cannot follow you
into that Fire.

If You Think that Love Is Great

If you think that love is great,
know this: the way God loves
is greater than what you can
ever imagine, and if you want
to find this love you must leap
over all you know and fall
into a love so deep and wide
that nothing else matters.

A Good Place to Start Again

If you want to be born again, look at those
who inspire you with their generosity, and
humble you with their compassion, and
try little by little to live like them—even if
you still clutch at chairs and lean against
walls like a child just learning to walk.

Go Deeper than This

If you want to go deeper than this, become
the love you desire, and risk saying Yes to love
in the midst of the injustices of this world
and in the face of the troubles that overwhelm
you. This is not the whole point of your life,
but it's a good place to start—again.

One Single One

This, I tell you, is true: in eternity, everything
is present at once, and everything is one,

for when God gazes upon God's self, God gazes
upon all that was and is and will be, looking and

seeing with a single eye, because when God
looks God sees all that is as one single One.

So if you want to see as God sees, look with
the same single eye, and when you do you

will see with the undivided eye of oneing love.

The Truth about Holiness

The truth about holiness
does not make it sound easy.
If you encounter an easy holiness,
run the other way.
Holiness comes from your being,
not from your works and doings.
Fast, rise early, pray, that's all fine,
but the more you embrace God
deep inside of you, the holier
you will become.

Becoming What You Love

A great teacher once said that the soul
becomes what it loves, so pay attention
to this and consider well what you love—
whether things that delight or inspire,
or those you feel drawn toward, for
while there's nothing wrong with any
of this, consider when you love that
you are becoming what you love, and
so love in a way that grows the soul and
gentles the mind and graces the world.
The rest will take care of itself.

Love Knows No Why

Love knows no Why, for if I love someone
because of what it brings me, I end up loving
only myself, but when I love another for
the goodness that is in them, I begin to love
without a Why. So devote yourself to this
whyless love, and seek the goodness that
is there in each and all, a light that ever burns,
however dimly, even in the darkest soul.

Out of Nothing

Some say we should give away what we have
to become free, which may be true, but if we
hold onto some part of ourselves and think
of this as an accomplishment, this is nothing
but blindness and stupidity, for then we have
only pretended to be poor and remain shackled
in our heart. So risk this: abandon yourself,
what you think you are and imagine you need
to be you, and dare to become the nothing
that God cannot resist who loves across
the distances and creates out of nothing.

So God Can Be God in You

If you want to be holy, do what is right
without seeking anything for it, until
you live your life without a single Why,
for if you are aware of what you hope
to receive for your holiness you will find
that there is no more than nothing, so try this:
work at becoming nothing when doing
what is good; disappear in your loving
so God can be God within you—and
make something new from this nothing.

Taking God with You

Taking God with you
is not for everyone.
Everyone can't. But
if you take God alone,
carrying nothing at all
but the One, you will
be taking God everywhere,
on the street, in the desert,
in the sanctuary, and
into your private room.

Possessing God

Possessing God
depends entirely
on the heart.
A sincere
and open heart
knows the real God,
and not
the imaginary one.

Become Love

If you want to know God,
become love. If you want
to know others, become love.
If you want to know yourself,
become love. And if you want
to know love, forget all you
thought you knew or needed
to know, and become love.

If You Keep Busy Thinking of Yourself

If you keep busy thinking of yourself, you will
know as much about God as the mouth knows
about color or the eye about taste. Think about it:
if you want to know God who is the whyless One,
try forgetting yourself, and when you do—even if
only for a single moment or for what is less than
a moment—you will possess all this One possesses.

A Deeper Stillness

We are too often unhappy, while on and on
the world remains the gift of presence God

meant it to be at the beginning and sustains
in every moment, and when we catch

even a glimpse of this, our restlessness
begins to open to a deeper stillness within us

where we will come to know that what is
now torn apart and broken will finally come

back to the stillness which rests in the deep
oneness of this life and in the breadth of love.

This Strange Land

When you find yourself possessed by God,
you will enter a strange land, a wilderness
which is nameless beyond names and more
unknown than known; there, you will find
that your I and God's I are a single I,
in the undivided unity of a whyless love.

Part Four

KNOWING NOTHING

Where Does This Leave Us?

God is a word
who speaks only
for himself.
You and every
other creature
wish to speak
for God, but you
can't, and if you
try, you best be
careful. Seriously,
be careful.

Eternal Life

So, you want eternal life?
What is the source of such a blessing?
What does Our Lord say, after all?
"Eternal life is for those who know God."
And how does that knowing take place?
I say, when the soul knows when she knows
the one, true God.

Do You Hear?

There is an
everlasting
wisdom here,
there, ready
for the hearing.
It abides, but only
for those souls
who are at home,
who are listening.

Stop Looking

Here is a truth that we can scarcely
imagine: where God is, there is the soul,
and where the soul is, there is God.

Think about it. When you do, you'll stop
looking for God here or there, now or then,
and pay attention to where you are and

who you are in your soul. Only then
will you finally see that the soul and
God are one. The rest will be easy.

Prayer for Knowing

Loving and merciful
One,
all truth,
allow me and
everyone who
prays these
words to
know what is
true. Amen.

Test for Divine Knowledge

Look at a stick
standing in water.
It appears bent
when it really is straight.
For me, it is enough
that what I know
of God is true in me,
and is true in God.

You say, I don't understand.

> I say
> the words
> aren't the
> problem.
> St. John
> begins
> his gospel
> with sublime
> and difficult
> matters of
> God
> and life.
> It is all
> good for you.

Free Your Mind, Now

The most powerful form of prayer of all
is the one that is free,
flowing from a mind unencumbered,
useful for the purpose,
waiting for reception,
awake.
Awake.

Give Up God

So you're still longing for God?
Your desire won't help you come
a single step closer. Give up your
desire, which won't help you—
and dare to give up God. Then
learn to make space in your mind
for the nothing God is, and find
that everything you need lies in
this nothingness. This is wisdom
truer and stronger than desire.

Don't Let Your Troubles Trouble You

Of course you have troubles.
Who doesn't?
Having troubles doesn't mean being bound by them,
or stuck with them.
Let your devotion to God be
free from these things,
immersed in God's preciousness—
those perfect intentions God has for your life.

What is the highest work of God?

It is simply this: giving birth.
Imagine this, then: God will not
rest until this birth happens—
in you. So don't get busy trying
to make something happen.
Relax. Let go of your need
to make something happen,
and open yourself to this birth;
the rest will come of itself.

How to Pray with Intensity

If you want to pray, really pray.
Then every part of your body,
ears, eyes, your heart,
and all your senses,
will join with your mouth,
and you won't stop until
you feel you're getting close
to being present to the One who is
already there, already praying.

No One Can Stop You

No one can stop you,
hinder, or disturb you,
if you are fixed on God alone.
For God is always at work
inside of you. And
what you do and say
will be godly,
so look out.

There Is Something Inside You

There is something inside you
that goes untouched by the world around you;
it is above and apart from the creature that you are.
Even angels don't have this something.
They are clear beings, deep and still, but without
the divine nature your soul possesses,
leaving it unlike anything else in this world.
Even angels.

Forget about Eternal Life

Our Lord says, If you give up everything for me,
you will receive eternal life; but if you give
everything up for the sake of eternal life,
you have given up nothing at all.
You have to give yourself up, and completely,
for to leave yourself behind is to be so ready
for heaven that the world no longer notices you.

Consider a Stone

Consider a stone,
how it falls,
easily,
freely.
Your praise
should so
move,
an inclination
to roll.

What do you think?

> That God has abandoned you,
> especially now?
> What person sees a friend
> in sorrow, pain, or loneliness
> without encouraging,
> without being near, present?
> Don't be foolish, my friend,
> God is here.

Try Desiring Nothing

If you think you can bargain with God,
offering your good works and best intentions
in the hope of some reward, think again:

these are like the doves sold in the temple,
whose sellers and buyers Jesus drove out
so long ago. Try this instead: desire nothing

and become like the unbounded Nothing,
which is neither here nor there. Only then,
in the Now of this Nothing, will you find

only God who wants your works of love
as an act of praise, and not your bargaining
for some reward beyond this great Nothing.

In God There Is Nothing but God

In God there is nothing but God,
and when you come to know

all creatures in this nothing,
you come to know the nothing

that is God. So try to know
creatures in the nothing beyond

every something, and there find
this nothing in every something,

which is God. You will either
understand this or you will not.

Breaking Through

When we give ourselves over to the depth of our perception,
we break through truth and goodness and come to know

God as God is in God's simple being; the wise teachers
tell us that when we do this, we grasp God beyond names;

but this is not enough, since even if we gain God in knowing,
we never grasp God in the ocean of what is and remains

undefinable in God; there, beyond perceiving and loving,
God is not this or that, neither here nor there; there, God

is mercy without reason or explanation, mercy all the way
from the beginning and mercy all the way, without end.

Wish to Understand

If you wish to understand God,
think about this: whatever you think
you know is not God, for God is
beyond knowing. So try
understanding God beyond
speech and without words.
How to do this? Sink down
into your you-ness, and so flow
into God's God-ness that your
you-ness and God's God-ness
become one mine.

God Doesn't Make People Sad

God doesn't make people sad,
yet happiness comes in
following the teaching,
"If any will come to me,
let them deny themselves."
This is a command, but also
a promise, a way to reward,
maybe suffering,
but to happiness, too,
that's true and lasting.

Let Go of Everything

Your soul is the highest temple where alone God dwells, higher
than everything on this earth, higher even than the angels.

Nothing but the soul—yes, your soul—is as high as God,
and as free. But to find God in this temple you must let go

of everything and cling to the Nothing that opens the door
to your soul, which alone among all created things is free.

Blessed Times of Trouble

Since God said,
"I am with you
in troubles,"
St. Bernard asked,
"Will you,
then,
please give
me trouble
all the time?"

Letting Go of It All

Do you wonder
how to know God,
how to hear God's word?
Let go of all you know,
all you hope for,
all you depend upon.
Only then will you
know the Word
that knows you,
and love the Love
that loves you, from
the beginning,
without end.

Less and More

If we were able to see God's goodness
as it truly is, we would know a mystery so great
and so mysterious that our minds
would not be able to take it in. And when
this happens, if it does, you won't
want to speak but will prefer to keep
silent about it, since it is a knowing
beyond words, because our words
are less than what it is, and our
knowing this is more than language.

Letting Go of Everything to Find God

If you desire to know God, let go of everything you
imagine you need, and turn from all you desire

and everything you will, for God is not in any of
these, not a single one—not even the best of all.

So stop your imagining, and let go of what you
want and think you need; when you've reduced

yourself to utter nothingness and given up all you
thought you were, then you'll be ready to taste

what this teaching of mine means, and know God
who is always waiting for you in nothingness.

Become One

What would it mean to risk trusting
that your happiness has *nothing* to do
with what you feel or know or think,
and everything to do with what you
do *not* feel or know or think?
Don't think about it, but become
one with your nothingness, amid
all that troubles you, and then you
will receive the rest—beyond all
you can imagine but not beyond
the one true love you desire.

A Great Overflowing

If you desire to know the immeasurable
sweetness of God, give up every hope
of deserving it, since this is beyond you;

instead, concentrate on making your soul
open to this gift, and when you do this God
cannot resist filling you to the point of

a great overflowing—which, once filled,
flows out to everything around you, until
it returns to the source from which all comes.

Do you think you can only find God in one way?

Then consider this: you cannot find God in any particular way, since God isn't bound to this way or that. So don't desire the way, but rather the One who *is* the way, and when you do this, you'll find that every way leads to God because every way *is* God. But you will only come to know this if you truly abandon yourself.

Do you think God can only find you in one way?

If so, consider this: what keeps us from God
is not what is outside of us, no matter how bad,
but the inner obstacles that we put in the way.
So guard yourself against yourself, and when
you do this you'll begin to see that whatever
way you follow, and whatever you like or dislike,
is all right.

If You Were Truly at Home in Yourself

If you were truly at home in yourself,
you would know that everything worth

saying is already deep within you but
must first be found there before it's

able to come forth as it wants to do,
and when you find it you begin to see

that all is finally one, and everything
is exactly what it is in itself and in God,

and you'll even begin to see how every
thing and everyone *is* God, and then

you'll come home to yourself in
all that was and is and will yet be.

Letting Go of My Self

I want to hold onto all that I have
and all that I am and hope to become,
and you invite me to let go of it all—

all the having and being and becoming—
and become the nothing that I am,
beyond all that I know and ever will

in this life, and when I free myself
of my self You cannot resist being
what is left in me, which is the true

self You gave me at the beginning.

This Single Path

There are as many ways
to be faithful as there are
roads to travel. Some are
crowded, others are less
travelled by, and what
matters is not to find
the best or even a better
one than where you are,
but to see that every way is
the right one if we open
ourselves to its gift.

Give Yourself to the One Way

I

Give yourself to the one way
that is yours, because God is
on this way, and little by
little you'll find you won't
miss out on anything on
this path—if you draw
all that is good into it.

II

And don't start off on one way
today, then look for a better one
tomorrow for fear you'll miss
out on something; rather, be-
come one with the One who is
the Way, and you'll not miss out
on a single thing, in whatever
way is yours to go.

A Hard but True Word

Here is a hard but true word: if we would grasp
what it means to love others as we love ourselves,

we must be ready to see everything that happens
to them as happening to us, because when all is

said and done there is nothing peculiar nor near
or far in human nature that is different than we

are in ourselves, and when we begin to live from
the heart of this truth, in the truth of our heart,

we find we cannot judge others or turn from them
in their suffering, even when it seems deserved,

for the same is happening to us and in us, as we
come to know when we love others as ourselves.

Lacking God Within

Lacking God within leads us to
seek everywhere without, and
in equal measure, to
discover what's missing.
But it won't work.
Places and people won't
lead us to God. We'll
imagine we're doing right, on
the road, even in church, but
it won't work.

Finding, Not Seeking

We usually miss You, cluttering our minds
with expectations about where and how
and who You are, but if we trust giving up
our seeking and let ourselves know You
in everything that is, even what's concealed
from us, we come to find You everywhere,
at all times and in an equal way, no
matter how strange this might seem to us.

An Imaginary God

An imaginary God
will please and delight you,
will satisfy and entice you,
but when your thoughts pass away,
this imaginary God
also disappears.
What you need is the
essential God within you,
not the imaginary one
on your lips.

If You Want to Be Perfect

If you want to be perfect, trust this:
turn from every "no" in your life
and free yourself of its cruel logic.

For if you make even a little room
for "no," you'll remain just who
you always were; you'll not change,

but will become like one who lives
in hell, which is the kingdom of "no,"
and there you'll fade away in fear.

God is not what you think

or even what you believe,
because God is
a word unspoken,
a thought unthought,
a belief unbelieved.
So if you wish to know
this God, practice wonder,
do what is good, and
cultivate silence.
The rest will follow.

Where Truth Dwells

Deep inside you,
in your innermost,
secret parts,
known only to
the Holy One
Who speaks with
you there,
is where you begin
eternal life.

Do You Want to Be Rich?

Cling, if you want, to things,
everywhere, that your
heart desires, but
where, then,
will your
heart
be?

Didn't you hear?
God has chosen the poor of this world,
rich in faith, to inherit the kingdom.

Part Five

EMBRACING EVERYTHING

Where Are You?

If I want to find God, I must give up thinking I know
where God is, or how I should find him, and give

myself to all the things in my life where God always
already is, and if I have God in this way I'll find

God in everything and miss God in nothing, for
God is in everything and misses nothing, and when

I find God in this way everything becomes God for me.

There is something in you
that is closer to God
than you can imagine
or understand and that
has nothing in common
with anyone or anything
else in this world or the next
or the next.

Worm in a Dung Heap

If I could discover myself
as I really am, united with God,
a creature bound to the uncreated,
even if for only a moment,
I would pay less attention
to the old me than I do
to a worm in a dung heap.

Horse in the Meadow

Have you seen how a horse,
on a summer's afternoon
in a wide green meadow,
gallops and dances and springs
about in the sun and wind?
This is just how God delights
in pouring himself into you.
Just like this!

The Suffering Man

Have you heard
about the man who
went to a holy father
to complain that
his sufferings were great?
Do you want me to ask
the Lord to take them from you?
the holy father asked.
No, not that, said the suffering man;
they are good for me;
but please intercede on my
behalf, and ask the Lord for just a
little more grace to
accompany them.

Nothing can be, unless You
    call it into being.
Nothing can survive, unless You
    will it to keep on going,
    says the Book of Wisdom.
So, is this Your desire?
Is this Your love?
It must be, and with Your love,
    the love that sustains everything,
    I know I will be fine.
If You take anything away, please
    not that love.

Where Is God?

Where is God?
you ask.
In here, over there,
let's not be silly.
This is beyond belief—
how the Word flows
in and flows out, how
God remains in all
things, and nothing,
and if you don't
understand, well
of course you don't,
don't be silly.

No Matter How Small

I
Whatever comes to God, no matter how small,
will be changed,
regardless

of how small or insignificant it is;
if we bring it to God, it can't be lost

and won't be squandered,
no matter how small.

II
For whatever is in God can't be
lost and won't be forgotten,

not remaining what it was but
becoming what it truly is—

no matter how small. If God
can do this with little things,

changing them from this into
what is divine, what more

will God do with your soul,
which bears his very image?

Where Is God's Temple?

There once was a meeting of theologians,
each one wiser than the others, gathered
to explain what God's true nature was.

One of the the wise ones argued that
God was in the soul, the soul in the heart—
so that God was most truly in the heart.

But I say this: the soul is entirely and
utterly present in every single part of
the body, even in the foot or in the eye.

If this is so, we must say that God is
present in every part of our body equally.
So take care of those toes of yours!

Christmas Poem

Why do we assume
that God became
human only once,
in the Incarnation?
Not so.
God becomes human
here and now just
as he did then.
Why is this?
So that he might
give birth to you,
too, as his only
begotten son.

Remember Who You Are, Now

A thought occurred one day to me.
Eckhart, you're a human being like everyone else.
But everyone else, even a cow,
sees and hears and chews the cud.
You, however, belong to no one
else but to God, who knows you better
than you know yourself.
Remember that.

You Cannot Believe

You cannot believe
how happy are all
who follow God
without regard
for reward,
rejoicing, in truth,
in simple things.
Such persons
live a good life,
Augustine says.

Consider those nets

the apostles
left behind
when Jesus
said,
"Follow me."
If your foot
were in the fire,
would you take
much time to
think before
you pulled
it out?

Everything Is God

I

What does our worth depend on? Not on what
we do or think, and not on what we make
of ourselves. It's like this: something as tiny
as a fly, in God, is of even more worth than
the highest angel. Ultimately, everything is,
in God, is one and of equal worth, since all
is one in God, which is to say one in love,
from the beginning and without end.

II

A wise master said this, but I would say
even more than this: *everything* is God,
nothing less or more than this. Why, then,
should it be different for you or for me,
since God made us not for ourselves but
for each other, all of us in God's image?
If you know this, live it; and, if you don't yet
know this, live it until you begin to do so.

Breaking Through It All

It all depends on an inner solitude that is ever
within us, in the midst of our crowded lives,

and when we find that solitude, regardless of where
we are or whom we are with, we begin to learn to
break through it all—whatever comes—and grasp
You in everything and allow You to take form in us,

in the midst of it all, as the One in our solitude.

A Little Castle

Know this truth: God is in you like
a little castle that rests in your soul,

greater than all you can imagine.
And this castle, which is God,

is so simple and one that in it
your very soul is one with God

and you yourself are finally
nothing but God.

God's Greening

I've said this many times before, but
it's so important that I want to say it

again: there is a power in the soul
that nothing can touch, nothing—

neither time nor the flesh; it flows
forth from the spirit within us, with-

out diminishing itself, and remains entire
despite its overflowing, and this power is

God's greening that blooms within us,
in all the joy and honor that God is.

You will know if God lives in you.

> The world will shine.
> Everything will take on divine savor.
> All will seem that God has
> taken shape, wherever you turn.
> And things which no longer concern you
> will become impressions of God.
> You will discover the image of
> what you love in each single thing.

Not of this World

This kingdom
where you now
find yourself
standing,
knows nothing
of your soul.
Who you really
are is not,
simply not,
of this world.

No Wonder

"Truth lives in us"
says Augustine,
and no wonder,
because it is God's
nature to be within.
This means that
your inner person,
quiet for God
alone,
is true and eternal.
No wonder.

Our Lord spoke

through the prophet:
"Nothing will satisfy me
but being aflame with love."
Then he prayed
to the Father that
we would be
more than united,
that we would be
One.

When we burn

> like a roaring fire,
> our wood
> changes from
> coarse wet
> and coldness
> into something
> entirely else,
> something created
> by that burn.

What satisfies the wood

is not heat.
A fire gives heat
to the wood
but it is not
heat that
satisfies it,
that calms,
silences,
and changes
the wood.
It is how fire
is born in it,
in its flaming
and light,
that satisfies
the wood
with a new
way of being.

What Should We Seek?

What should we seek?
To love justice and keep it.

And when we love, what
should we love? God,

without any idea or
expectation about

what or who God is.
And what will all this

seeking give us but
ourselves as we truly are,

bound with the One
who is Love unbounded.

All or Nothing

So you want to find God? Give up thinking you
know where to look, or how to think about God

for if you imagine tasting God in only one way,
you'll remain small in your thinking and cold in

your living. But if you want to find God in the right
way, expect to find him in everything in your life—

in difficulties and in comforts, in tears and in joy.
For if you seek God only in one thing, you'll find

him in no thing, for God is in all that is. But you
must first change to know what this means.

Before you light

you'll crackle
and hiss.
You'll smoke
and fight.
You'll struggle
and doubt.

But then you
may find the fire
has made you
warm,
and you'll
go silent.

Pushing God under a Bench

If you want to know God in this way or in that,
beware, for your desire for such a narrow way

separates you from God by binding you to your
own opinions, pushing God under a bench.

For you're the cause of the obstacles you find
in your life, so guard yourself against yourself,

and open your heart to the love that is present
to you in darkness and light, in sorrow and joy.

Take Good Care

Take good care
of what is good
in your life.
Use it well.

Know that all goodness
is on loan to you
from God,
only for a time.

As the sun lends light
to the world,
goodness can set
at the end of day.

Some truths are utterly simple

yet no less amazing for that.
Here's one: if you let go

of your will, if even for
a moment, all the time

you've wasted, all the time
you've lost, will finally

become present to you
in that very moment.

St. Antony fought devils

in the desert, alone.
They abused and debased
this man of holiness
who, when he finally sent
them packing, gasped,
"Where were you, God?"
"Right here," came back.

Be careful to remember your God

in those moments
when you leave the lovely quietude
of your private cell
or sanctuary.
Where do you go, then?
Into the crowd with its bustle and anger.
Who are you, then?

Even in You

Try to imagine this, if you can:
God did not create once, before
time, but is always creating,
all the time and in every place,
even in you, and try to comprehend
this truth that is astonishing and
finally beyond belief:
               that God
is in all things, but the more
God is in things the more God
is outside them—the more in,
the more out, and the more out,
the more in. This is how God
is in you, creating even now
as at the beginning, and is
never finished, without end.

The Annunciation

As a great prince will send his attendants ahead
to arrange only the very best accommodations,

so with the advent of the Word of God, which
came into this world many, many years ago,

announced and arranged by a heavenly attendant—
the angel who visited Mary—selecting for his Lord

the finest accommodations of all.

At the Heart of Everything

I
Too often we look on the surface
of things, and when we do we fail

to see that each one mirrors some
measure of the immeasurable good

that is in God and is God, and until
we begin to see this we remain

restless and unsatisfied.

II
But when we do we begin to glimpse
something of the image in which God

created all that was and is and will be,
then we taste the solitude at the heart

of everything and everyone—that is,
God—and know that in this unity no

one creature is better than another.

If God be in you

    it did not happen by some act of will.
        You cannot.
    It did not take place by force of intellect.
        Don't strain yourself.
    Every veil was removed for God to be in you,
        in the nakedness of your soul.

So You Want to Find God?

Then don't imagine you know
where to look, because all things
are God's speech—that stone lying
on the path no less than the birds
of the air or the angels of heaven,
each speaking in its own way
of the One who made it.
So listen to everything, even
the unspeaking rocks, and learn
what it is to speak of God with
a speech beyond words.

The Mystery that Won't Always Be

Some will say,
this can't be true,
at least not yet.
I'll remind them
that God has
already created everything,
even what is to come—
what we often call the future.
All will become clear
in the years ahead.
I can't help it if they
can't see.

Epilogue: Come Home to Yourself

If you want to discover the truth about God,
don't strive for things that lie beyond you.

Draw your thoughts inward to the center, and
seek to become one and simple in your soul.

Let go of all that distracts you, all you desire,
and come home to yourself, and when you do,

you'll become the truth you first sought.

Notes and Sources for the Poems

Sources

In the notes to the poems, references to various collections of Eckhart's sermons and writings are indicated as follows:

Deutsche Predigten
Meister Eckehart: Deutsche Predigten und Traktate. Edited and
translated into modern German by Josef Quint. Munich:
Carl Hanser Verlag, 1979.

Einheit im Sein
Meister Eckhart: Einheit im Sein und Wirken. Translated, edited,
and introduced by Dietmar Mieth. Munich and Zurich: R.
Piper, 1986.

Essential Sermons
*Meister Eckhart: The Essential Sermons, Commentaries, Treatises,
and Defense.* Translated into English and Introduced by
Edmund Colledge, OSA, and Bernard McGinn. New York:
Paulist Press, 1981.

Selected Writings
Meister Eckhart: Selected Writings. Selected and translated into English by Oliver Davies. London: Selected Writings Books, 1994.

Teacher and Preacher
Meister Eckhart: Teacher and Preacher. Edited and translated into English by Bernard McGinn, with the Collaboration of Frank Tobin and Elvira Borgstadt. New York: Paulist Press, 1986.

Treatises and Sermons
of Meister Eckhart. Selected and translated from Latin and German by James M. Clark and John V. Skinner. New York: Harper & Brothers, 1958.

Poems, with references
[in the order in which they appear]

There Is a Secret Hidden in the Heart; see *Teacher and Preacher*, 285.

PART ONE. SEEKING LIGHT

Even in the Shadows; see *Selected Writings*, 103.

God Is Green; see *Selected Writings*, 161.

If You Could See; see *Selected Writings*, 161.

God's Now; see *Selected Writings*, 161.

The Inner Eye; see *Selected Writings*, 173.

Just for a Moment; see *Selected Writings*, 166.

God's Gaze; see *Selected Writings*, 174.

A Great Light; see *Teacher and Preacher*, 171, with reference to
    Wisdom 18:1,14.

Received; see *Teacher and Preacher*, 228.

Follow Me; see *Treatises and Sermons*, 176, with reference to
    Jn. 1:43.

To Be Satisfied with Hell; see *Teacher and Preacher*, 269.

Did You Ever Wonder; see *Deutsche Predigten*, 189–90.

Rotten Eggs and Brown Apples; see *Treatises and Sermons*, 176.

An Honest Prayer; see *Treatises and Sermons*, 176.

Intentions Matter; see *Treatises and Sermons*, 178.

Yes, Darkness; see *Essential Sermons*, 150–51.

Ours Is the Darkness; see *Essential Sermons*, 148–49.

The Sheep's Eye and Mine; see *Essential Sermons*, 198.

Seek God in Nothing; see *Teacher and Preacher*, 323.

Pay Attention to the Nothing; see *Teacher and Preacher*, 320.

Find the Inner Eye ; see *Deutsche Predigten*, 203.

If You Want to Reach the Highest Wisdom; see *Essential
    Sermons*, 197.

Becoming Peace; see *Deutsche Predigten*, 214–15.

Think Again; see *Essential Sermons*, 148–49.

A Wide Wilderness; see *Selected Writings*, 173.

Enclosed; see *Selected Writings*, 167.

Four Kinds of Ecstasy; see *Treatises and Sermons*, 207, with
    reference to Gen. 2:21 and the four-fold ecstasy of
    St. Thomas Aquinas's *De Veritate*.

What You Know with God; see *Treatises and Sermons*, 208.

PART TWO. FACING DARKNESS

To Someone with God; see *Selected Writings*, 119.

Where We Are; see *Selected Writings*, 160.

Blessed Are the Martyrs; see *Selected Writings*, 165.

Between Two Darknesses; see *Essential Sermons*, 196.

No Matter How Deep the Darkness; see *Essential Sermons*, 198.

Picture the Knight; see *Selected Writings*, 93.

Whatever It Is; see *Teacher and Preacher*, 213.

Try Emptying Yourself; see *Selected Writings*, 123-24.

If You Want to Find the Truth; see *Selected Writings*, 136–37.

If We Could Ever See; see *Deutsche Predigten*, 162.

Your Notebook Jottings; see *Teacher and Preacher*, 228.

A Mirror; see *Teacher and Preacher*, 258.

In Dark Times; see *Deutsche Predigten*, 192.

We Cannot Know What God Is; see *Deutsche Predigten*, 160–62.

Some Imagine There Is No Light; see *Selected Writings*, 216–17.

Anger or Peace?; see *Essential Sermons*, 207.

Learn to Become God's Joy; see *Deutsche Predigten*, 172–73.

This Truth Is All that Matters; see *Selected Writings*, 136–37.

....

     (Sources for Poems on pp. 39–51)

One Love; see *Deutsche Predigten*, 180–81.

Among the Miracles; see *Deutsche Predigten*, 162.

If You Were So Holy; see *Selected Writings*, 9-10.

Who Can Understand This; see *Selected Writings*, 123–24.

Some Say God Is Gentle; see *Selected Writings*, 176–77.

If It Is True; see *Selected Writings*, 170–72.

Imagine this Amazing Truth; see *Selected Writings*, 170–72.

You Ask, What Is Evil?; see *Treatises and Sermons*, 196.

Removals; see *Treatises and Sermons*, 199.

Your pride, Eckhart; see *Treatises and Sermons*, 200.

PART THREE. RISKING LOVE

May I Be Struck Dead; see *Teacher and Preacher*, 336.

Gather the Treasure; see *Teacher and Preacher*, 344.

Sleep for a Century; see *Spiritual Writings*, 124.

We Are All Virginal; see *Selected Writings*, 159.

You Should Really Know; see *Selected Writings*, 7.

May Your Will Be Done; see *Spiritual Writings*, 124.

This Is God's Prayer; see *Selected Writings*, 118.

Sweet Fruit; see *Selected Writings*, 119.

An Angel's Joy; see *Teacher and Preacher*, 269.

Why Love Is Best; see *Teacher and Preacher*, 212, reflecting on
     Ex. 3:14 and 1 Jn. 4:8.

The Best Thing about Love; see *Einheit im Sein*, 82–84.

Heavenly Now; see *Treatises and Sermons*, 199, with reference
     to 2 Cor. 4:16.

God Is Not to Be Found in Any Way, see *Deutsche Predigten*,
     196.

Pray for Me; see *Deutsche Predigten*, 181.

. . . .

(Sources for Poems on pp. 66–77)

The soul that is yours; see *Teacher and Preacher*, 213-14.

One in the One; see *Deutsche Predigten*, 190.

Have You Tasted?; see *Treatises and Sermons*, 187, with Eckhart paraphrasing both Sts. John Chrysostom and Augustine.

What We Love We Become in Love; see *Deutsche Predigten*, 174.

Why Would You?; see *Treatises and Sermons*, 184-85.

The Value of Gold; see *Teacher and Preacher*, 250.

What Is Freedom?; see *Deutsche Predigten*, 183–87.

God Is Not Far Away; see *Book of Divine Consolation*, I in Clark / Skinner

Solomon Says; see *Selected Writings*, 124, with reference to Ecc. 1:7.

How Should We Seek God? I; see *Teacher and Preacher*, 340–41.

How Should We Seek God? II; see *Teacher and Preacher*, 341.

Forget about Being Spiritual; see *Essential Sermons*, 208.

There Is a Comfort in Suffering?; see *Treatises and Sermons*, 111-12.

This is difficult, Eckhart; see *Treatises and Sermons*, 113.

Don't Be Like King David; see *Treatises and Sermons*, 116.

Into the Fire; see *Treatises and Sermons*, 124-25.

If You Think that Love Is Great; see *Selected Writings*, 209–10.

A Good Place to Start Again; see *Selected Writings*, 101–02.

Go Deeper than This; see *Selected Writings*, 101–02.

One Single One; see *Deutsche Predigten*, 174.

The Truth about Holiness; from *Selected Writings*, 7.

Becoming What You Love; see *Selected Writings*, 116.

Love Knows No Why; see *Selected Writings*, 119.

Out of Nothing; see *Selected Writings*, 120.

So God Can Be God in You; see *Selected Writings*, 145.

Taking God with You; see *Selected Writings*, 9.

Possessing God; see *Selected Writings*, 10.

Become Love; see *Selected Writings*, 150–51.

If You Keep Busy Thinking of Yourself; see *Selected Writings*,
122.

A Deeper Stillness; see *Deutsche Predigten*, 166–67.

This Strange Land; see *Selected Writings*, 122.

PART FOUR. KNOWING NOTHING

Where Does This Leave Us?"; see *Spiritual Writings*, 128.

Eternal Life; see *Spiritual Writings*, 107, with reference to
Jn. 17:3.

Do You Hear?; see *Selected Writings*, 175.

Stop Looking; see *Deutsche Predigten*, 206-07.

....

Prayer for Knowing; see *Spiritual Writings*, 95.

Test for Divine Knowledge; see *Selected Writings*, 94.

You say, I don't understand; see *Selected Writings*, 95.

Free Your Mind, Now; see *Selected Writings*, 4-5.

Give Up God, see *Deutsche Predigten*, 58–62.

Don't Let Your Troubles Trouble You; see *Selected Writings*, 5.

What is the highest work of God?; see *Deutsche Predigten*, 208.

How to Pray with Intensity; see *Selected Writings*, 5.

No One Can Stop You; see *Selected Writings*, 9.

There Is Something Inside You; see *Spiritual Writings*, 121.

Forget about Eternal Life; see *Selected Writings*, 120, with
reference to Mt. 19:29.

Consider a Stone; see *Treatises and Sermons*, 130.

What do you think?; see *Treatises and Sermons*, 138.

(Sources for Poems on pp. 116–128)

Try Desiring Nothing; see *Deutsche Predigten*, 154-55.

In God There Is Nothing but God; see *Teacher and Preacher*, 323.

Breaking Through; see *Deutsche Predigten*, 189–90.

Wish to Understand; see *Essential Sermons*, 207.

God Doesn't Make People Sad; see *Treatises and Sermons*, 135-36.

Let Go of Everything; see *Deutsche Predigten*, 156.

Blessed Times of Trouble; see *Treatises and Sermons*, 139, with reference to Bernard's sermon 17 on The Psalms.

Letting Go of It All; see *Deutsche Predigten*, 213–14.

Less and More; see *Spiritual Writings*, 136–37.

Letting Go of Everything to Find God; see *Deutsche Predigten*, 205.

Become One; see *Spiritual Writings*, 104.

....

A Great Overflowing; see *Deutsche Predigten*, 158.

Do you think you can only find God in one way?; see *Spiritual Writings*, 190–91.

Do you think God can only find you in one way?; see *Spiritual Writings*, 190–91.

If You Were Truly at Home in Yourself; see *Deutsche Predigten*, 170–71.

Letting Go of My Self; see *Spiritual Writings*, 41–42.

This Single Path; see *Spiritual Writings*, 43.

Give Yourself to the One Way; see *Spiritual Writings*, 43.

A Hard but True Word; see *Deutsche Predigten*, 175.

Lacking God Within; see *Treatises and Sermons*, 69.

Finding, Not Seeking; see *Spiritual Writings*, 13.

Imaginary God; see *Treatises and Sermons*, 69.

(Sources for Poems on pp. 140–150)

If You Want to Be Perfect; see *Deutsche Predigten*, 179–80.

God is not what you think; see ESCTD 203–204

Where Truth Dwells; see *Treatises and Sermons*, 201.

Do You Want to Be Rich?; see *Treatises and Sermons*, 201.

PART FIVE. EMBRACING EVERYTHING

Where Are You?; see *Spiritual Writings*, 9.

Worlds Forever; see *Selected Writings*, 177.

Worm in a Dung Heap; see *Selected Writings*, 177.

Horse in the Meadow; see *Selected Writings*, 178.

The Suffering Man; see *Selected Writings*, 91.

Survival Notes; see *Spiritual Writings*, 92, with reference to
    Book of Wisdom 11:25.

Where Is God?; see *Spiritual Writings*, 123.

No Matter How Small; see *Deutsche Predigten*, 167.

Where Is God's Temple?; see *Deutsche Predigten*, 196.

Christmas Poem; see Spiritual Writings, 124.

Remember Who You Are, Now; see *Selected Writings*, 121.

You Cannot Believe; see *Treatises and Sermons*, 179.

Consider those nets; see *Treatises and Sermons*, 179.

Everything Is God; see *Deutsche Predigten*, 213–17.

Breaking Through It All; see *Spiritual Writings*, 11.

A Little Castle; see *Deutsche Predigten*, 164.

God's Greening; see *Deutsche Predigten*, 161.

You will know if God lives in you; see *Treatises and Sermons*, 70.

Not of This World; see *Treatises and Sermons*, 195.

No Wonder; *Treatises and Sermons*, 201.

Our Lord Spoke; see *Treatises and Sermons*, 125.

When we burn; see *Treatises and Sermons*, 125.

What satisfies the wood; see *Treatises and Sermons*, 125-26.

What Should We Seek?; see *Deutsche Predigten*, 186–87.

All or Nothing; see *Deutsche Predigten*, 176.

Before you light; see *Treatises and Sermons*, 125-26.

Pushing God under a Bench; see *Deutsche Predigten*, 177.

Take Good Care; see *Treatises and Sermons*, 128.

Some truths are utterly simple; see *Deutsche Predigten*, 181.

St. Antony fought devils; see *Treatises and Sermons*, 137-38.

Be careful to remember your God; see *Treatises and Sermons*, 68-69.

Even in You; see *Spiritual Writings*, 122–23.

The Annunciation; see *Treatises and Sermons*, 188.

. . . .

At the Heart of Everything; see *Deutsche Predigten*, 166–67.

If God be in you; see *Treatises and Sermons*, 194-95.

So You Want to Find God?; see *Essential Sermons*, 205.

The Mystery that Won't Always Be; see *Selected Writings*, 94.

Come Home to Yourself, *Deutsche Predigten*, 213.

INDEX OF POEMS

ABOUT THE AUTHORS

MARK S. BURROWS, poet and professor of religion and literature at the Protestant University of Applied Sciences in Bochum, Germany, is a scholar of medieval theology, with a particular interest in Christian mysticism. His recent volume of poems, *The Chance of Home*, was published in 2018, and he is the recipient of the Witter Bynner Prize in Poetry as well as an invited member of the *Bochumer Literaten*, a group of professional writers in Germany. His interest in German literature led to his translation of Rainer Maria Rilke's *The Book of Hours* (published as *Prayers of a Young Poet*, 2016) and a collection of poems by the German-Iranian poet SAID, *99 Psalms*. He edits poetry for Paraclete Press as well as the journals *Spiritus* and *Arts*, and is married and the father of two daughters, dividing his time between Bochum and Camden, Maine.

JON M. SWEENEY is one of religion's most respected writers. His medieval history, *The Pope Who Quit*, was published by Random House and optioned by HBO. He is also author of many books on Francis of Assisi, including *When Saint Francis Saved the Church*, winner of a Catholic Press Association award, and *Francis of Assisi in His Own Words*, a collection of primary texts popular on college campuses. A new fiction series for young readers, *The Pope's Cat*, began to appear in 2018. He has been interviewed on *CBS Saturday Morning*, Fox News, *Religion and Ethics Newsweekly*, and on the popular nightly program, *Chicago Tonight*. Sweeney is the publisher at Paraclete Press. He writes regularly for *America* and *The Tablet* (UK), is married, the father of four, and lives in Milwaukee, Wisconsin.

HAMPTON ROADS PUBLISHING COMPANY

. . . for the evolving human spirit

Hampton Roads Publishing Company publishes books on a variety of subjects, including spirituality, health, and other related topics.

For a copy of our latest trade catalog, call (978) 465-0504 or visit our distributor's website at *www.redwheelweiser.com*. You can also sign up for our newsletter and special offers by going to *www.redwheelweiser.com/newsletter/*.